Islamic Beginnings
Part 3

In honor of my parents.

Yusufali Nafsi & Farzana Nafsi

May they rest in peace. Request for Surah Al-Fatihah.

By Tabassum Nafsi

بِسْمِ اللهِ الرَّحْمٰنِ الرَّحِيْمِ

In the name of Allah,
the Most Beneficent; the Most Merciful

Prophet Muhammad (saww) said: “I am leaving behind me two very weighty things for you. So long as you will remain connected with them you will never go astray after my departure and they (the two things) are heavier than one another.

One of them is the Book of Allah (Quran) and it is a rope which hangs from the heavens to the earth and the other is my progeny, my Ahl al-Bayt (as)."

As Muslim, it is important that we follow the message given to us by Allah and follow the path shown to us by Prophet Muhammad (saww).

Tawhid

There is only one Allah.

We are all His creation.

He is our creator.

He created everything in this universe.

He has no partner.

He is our Sustainer

He is the only one worthy of our worship.

We must submit to Him.

Circle the things created by Allah.

Islam

Unlike animals, Allah gave human beings intelligence and wisdom so we can think and learn.

This intelligence makes us superior to any other being in the universe.

Then Allah sent us His message—the religion of Islam for all of mankind.

Islam teaches us moral values.

Islam teaches us good manners.

Islam teaches us respect.

Islam teaches us humility.

Islam teaches us the difference between right and wrong: Haram and Halal.

Fill in the blanks by unscrambling the words.

I am a ________________. (S L I M U M)

I believe there is only ________________ Allah. (E N O)

Muhammad (saww) is our Last ________________. (P H T E R O P)

Islam means ________________. (E P C A E)

Islam teaches ________________ values. (O O D G)

Faith and the Right of Others

Intelligence is the foundation of faith. Faith means having a strong belief in Allah and His doctrine. Everything in this universe is a testament to His existence.

"Indeed, between heavens and the earth, are signs for the believers."
Quran 45:3

A Muslim believes that Allah is watching his actions; as a result, he or she refrains from bad deeds.

Islam also lays a lot of significance on the rights of other human beings. These are known as, "Huquq – al- Ibad." Taking care of neighbors, tending to the sick, feeding the poor, being generous, kindness to children and women are characteristics of a good Muslim.

Adhan (Call to Prayer)

4x
الله اكبر
Allah is great

2x
اشهد ان لا اله الا الله
I testify that there is no god but Allah.

2x
اشهد ان محمدا رسول الله
I testify that Muhammad (saww) is the Messenger of Allah.

2x
اشهد ان عليا ولي الله
I testify that Ali (as) is the wali of Allah

2x
حي على الصلاة
Hasten to Pray (salah)

2x
حي على الفلاح
Hasten to Salvation.

2x
حي على خير العمل
Hasten to the Best deeds.

2x
الله اكبر
Allah is great.

2x
لا اله الا الله
There is no god but Allah.

Good Deeds

Work Hard

Respect Your Elders

Stay Clean

Be Honest

Help Others

Be Fair

Good Habits

Sleep Early

Respect Your Teachers

Give Charity

Say Salam

Love Your Family

Thank Allah

Find the hidden objects

Prophet Muhammad al-Mustafa (saww)

He was born in Mecca.

He was born on 17th Rabi al-Awwal.

He died on 28th Safar.

His father's name was Abdullah and his mother's name was Aaminah.

He was raised by his uncle, Abu Talib (as).

He married Lady Khadijah (sa) at the age of 25. Lady Khadijah (sa) was a successful businesswoman. After her marriage to the Prophet Muhammad (saww), she helped him financially in the propagation of Islam. She was known for her generosity and human welfare.

He is buried in Medina.

He is the last messenger of Allah.

ALLAH calls Prophet Muhammad (saww) by many names.

Quran calls him as

Taha

Yasin

Aula (Most Worthy)

Aziz (Noble)

People of Mecca called Prophet Muhammad (Saww):

Sadiq which means, “Honest.”

Ameen which means, “Trustworthy.”

Muhammad (saww) was an ideal man and a role model for all humans. He is also called: “Rahmatun lil Alameen.” It means: A Mercy for all of Creation.

Lady Fatimah Zahra (sa)

She is the only child of the Prophet Muhammad (saww).

She is the "Chief of the Women of Paradise."

Narration: I never saw anyone who resembled the Messenger of Allah in his gestures or manners more than his daughter Fatimah. When she came to visit him, he would stand and kiss her, and sit her down in his place.

She was known in Mecca to be a radiant pearl of knowledge, of piety and of virtue.

Prophet Muhammad (saww) said: "O Fatimah! Indeed, Allah is angered for your anger, and is pleased for your pleasure."

Ayah al-Tathir

"Verily, Allah intends but to keep off from you (every kind of) uncleanliness, O you the people of the House, and purify you (with) a thorough purification." (33:33)

The Hadith of the Cloak (Hadith al-Kisa) refers to the Ahl al-Kisa. The hadith is an account of an incident where Prophet Muhammad (saww) gathered Hasan, Husayn, Ali, and Fatimah under his cloak and called them his "Ahl al-Bayt – meaning "The People of the House" and then Allah sent this verse to honor them.

Tasbih of Fatimah (sa)

Once upon a time, Lady Fatimah (sa) approached her father, Prophet Muhammad (saww), as she was suffering from hardship of her daily routine. She intended to ask him for a servant to help her with her household chores.

Prophet Muhammad (saww) replied: “Can I give you something better?” She replied: “Yes!”

So, he gave her a precious gift in the form of a tasbih. He asked her to recite this.

34 times – Allahu Akbar (Allah is the Greatest)

33 times – Alhamdulillah (Praise be to Allah)

33 times- Subhan Allah (Glory to be Allah)

Prophet Muhammad (saww) was known for his good manners and kind heart .

Some people of Mecca were mean to him and would call him names after his son died. They happily imagined that with the demise of the Holy Prophet (saww), the message from Allah would cease to exist.

When they made fun of Prophet Muhammad (saww), Allah revealed Surah al-Kauthar. It was an answer to the enemies of the apostle to inform them that Islam and the Quran would remain and ceaselessly continue, forever.

It is believed that al-Kauthar means existence of Lady Fatimah Zahra (sa). The family of Prophet Muhammad (saww) are known as the, "Ahl al-Bayt."

Surah al-Kauthar

إِنَّا أَعْطَيْنَاكَ الْكَوْثَرَ ﴿١﴾

Indeed We have given you, [O Muhammad], Al-Kauthar

فَصَلِّ لِرَبِّكَ وَانْحَرْ ﴿٢﴾

So pray to your Lord and sacrifice

إِنَّ شَانِئَكَ هُوَ الْأَبْتَرُ ﴿٣﴾

Indeed, your enemy is the one cut off

Ahl al-Kisa (Panjatan)

The five-beloved people of Allah.

They are the family of Lady Fatimah (sa)

Prophet Muhammad (saww)

Imam Ali (as)

Lady Fatimah (sa)

Imam Hasan (as)

Imam Husayn (as)

Panjatan

Five, five, five,
Panjatan are five,
The blessed masumeen,
They are the five!

Family of Muhammad,
and Fatimah,
Under the kisa,
They are the five!

Muhammad and Ali,
Ya Fatimah!
Hasan and Husayn
They are the five!

Our problems go away,
When we say their names,
They show us the "ray"
When we follow their way!

Five, five, five,
Panjatan are five,
The blessed masumeen,
They are the five!

Poem credit: Tazeen Abbas

Famous Sayings by Prophet Muhammad (saww)

No honor is nobler than humility and kindness.

The one who brushes his teeth twice a day has kept alive the sunnah of the prophets.

Cleanliness is half of faith.

Strive always to excel in virtue and truth.

The strongest among you is the one who controls his anger.

Famous Sayings by Imam Ali (as)

Knowledge is power.

Only rely upon Allah.

Pride cuts the path to success.

Jealousy is a sickness.

Subdue your anger and forgive a guilty person while you are in power.

Find the names of the Ahl al-Kisa (Panjatan)

F	A	T	I	M	A	H	S	I
D	C	A	E	N	O	A	M	L
W	B	L	A	R	U	S	Q	C
C	B	I	A	B	I	A	H	T
R	H	U	S	A	Y	N	D	Q
C	M	U	H	A	M	M	A	D

Dua

رَبِّ زِدْنِي عِلْمًا

O Lord, increase my knowledge. Quran 20:114

رَبَّنَا آتِنَا فِي الدُّنْيَا حَسَنَةً وَفِي الْآخِرَةِ حَسَنَةً وَقِنَا عَذَابَ النَّارِ

Our Lord, give us good in this world, and good in the hereafter, and save us from the torment of fire. Quran 2:201

CPSIA information can be obtained
at www.ICGtesting.com
Printed in the USA
LVHW071035100223
738879LV00029B/353